The Four Principles of Happy Cash Flow™

By

Leita Hart, CPA

Published by

Fanta Sea Publishing

Copyright © 2004

Leita Hart

International Standard Book Number: 1-59196-484-9

Produced in U.S. by InstantPublisher.com

Dedicated to Sara,
my precious daughter
who lights a fire under me.

The Four Principles of Happy Cash Flow™

By Leita Hart, CPA

Contents

Introduction: A Beginner's Hard-Earned Wisdom

A few years ago, a friend of mine who is an engineer left his corporate job and started his own company with four other engineers. They were all very smart about their product — global positioning systems — but had little experience in or knowledge of how a business works. As a matter of fact, my friend's business title was *Engineer in Charge of Finance and Administration*.

Well, after much suffering, he approached me to get some help. His partners were confused and frustrated because they never seemed to have enough cash in the business bank account when payroll time rolled around, and they had to contribute their personal cash to cover it. They argued that they had just made a tremendous sale to the Coast Guard for over $200,000. How could they possibly be short on cash? What had my friend, the *Engineer in Charge of Finance*, done with the money?

After asking my friend a few questions I began to get a picture of what had happened to his cash. He was experiencing what many businesses experience when they either take their eyes off of, or don't understand, cash flow. The reason I wrote this book is to help business owners, managers and employees understand the impact of their decisions on the lifeblood of the business — cash!

After a little coaching, my friend was able to figure out what to do and not do in his business. He began to watch cash and the things that impacted cash much more closely. He was able to explain to his partners what had happened and what would happen given any decision they made in the future.

He did so well in fact, that a competitor recently bought his company. My friend is now a millionaire living a quiet life on the Texas coast — fishing! Let's learn how he did it and what to look out for.

Chapter 1: Generating Your Own Cash Flow

Would you say that your business is a cash-generating machine or that it is in a cash-consuming vacuum? Is your business flexible and lean or rigid and wasteful? Or is your business somewhere in between?

Cash is the most powerful business asset you can have and there are many ways to get it. Some ways are wiser than others. You can sell a piece of your business and with it a share of profits and a share of control over your business.

Or you could get a loan. A loan obligates you to pay interest and principle on a set schedule . . . and you may also have to give up some control in your business.

Or you can generate cash by using my personal favorite technique — make it yourself by the wise application of four key principles.

Application of these principles can give your company new strength and possibly turn it into the cash-generating machine you always thought it could be!

What Is So Great About Generating Your Own Cash Flow?

It is all about control and self-sufficiency. Think about it from a personal level — you don't want to have to get a loan from your Aunt Harriet to pay your rent, or sell your body parts to science in order to generate cash. After a while, those resources are likely to exhaust themselves. But if you have a job or another source of income that you control, you get to say what goes. Same thing for a corporation: it is best if the company can control its own destiny.

What benefits do you derive from additional cash flow? You can:

- Pay your payroll

- Reduce your debt

- Buy back the ownership of your company from shareholders

- Take more cash home

- Take advantage of unique opportunities

- Have more business fun

Cash flow gives you flexibility and strength.

 Imagine having $100,000 cash in your pocket today. You could go out and have a really good time! But, if you have that same $100,000 tied up in your house, then you should enjoy watching cable TV . . . because that may be all that you will be doing today.

Cash gives you the flexibility to act. If a competitor comes out with a new product or service, and they are making good money with it, you can add the product or service to your repertoire fast. If you do not have the cash, you may first have to go find someone to loan you the money or sell a piece of your business. Or, worst yet, you may have to let the opportunity go.

In most industries, change is rapid. Cash gives you the ability to flow with that change and not get stuck.

And cash gives you strength because it lets you withstand market fluctuations. As I write, the economy in my hometown — Austin, Texas — is slowing. Some businesses, which were short on cash, are going under; some are laying off employees; and some are telling their employees that they can't travel or attend training. But one of the leaders in this town, Dell Computer, is strengthening its market position because it has extra cash and its competitors don't.

Dell Computer is one of the best managers of cash around. They are a cash-generating machine.

What Dell is able to do, that some of its competitors cannot, is withstand the slowdown in PC sales while keeping their prices consistently low. They have a huge cash reserve that they made by managing their cash and working capital well . . . so they can last and last while their competitors suffer. An interesting scenario.

And Dell is not the only company smart about cash flow. Wal-Mart also has a great technique for managing cash flow, as do several other businesses we will look at later.

The Four Principles of Happy Cash Flow™

The Four Principles of Happy Cash Flow™ can and should be applied to any business. We are going to start by applying these principles to Dell Computer, but as we go through the principles, please keep your own business in mind. And although Dell is a manufacturing-type business, we can and later *will* apply these principles to other types, including service businesses.

As you read, ask yourself how your business stacks up. Think of what you could do to improve your cash flow.

Chapter 2:
The First Principle of
Happy Cash Flow™

The first principle is best illustrated by a story, and it is the story of the Fuller Brush Man.

The Fuller Brush Company started at the turn of the last century. The Fuller Brush Man had a very simple business, but the way he set up his cash flow was very, very smart.

What he did was get his brooms and his mops and his brushes on credit from his suppliers. He would make agreements to pay them back in 30 days. And then he would take this stuff he didn't even own, the brooms, mops, and brushes, and sell them door-to-door for cash. Taking something you don't even own and selling it for cash is illegal in most cases — it is called "fencing." But you can get away with a version of it in business without worrying about jail.

This is the perfect cash flow scenario, because he never had to reach into his own pocket to finance his operations. He was using the suppliers' money AND the customers' money to run his business.

He sold the supplier's goods, goods the Fuller Brush Company didn't even own, and paid the supplier for it later.

He didn't let his *customers* have credit, however. He collected cash from them immediately. This way he was always a few days ahead of the game.

**So the First Principle
of Happy Cash Flow™ is
Use Other People's Money**

How *Not* to Do It

Let's talk about the first principle in more detail. The example of the business I am using for this diagram is a manufacturing operation. Your business may not be a manufacturing operation . . . but not to fear . . . we will cover other types of businesses after we have a chance to touch on the four principles.

So, let us pretend that we are a traditionally run manufacturing operation. The method described below is an OK way to run your business, but not the best application of our first principle.

The first thing you do as a traditional manufacturer is *buy raw inventory on credit* from your suppliers. Let's say you make computers — you would be buying the components of the computer such as the memory and box to put it in.

Next you will assemble or *manufacture* the computer.

Next you will *store* the finished computers as they wait to be sold.

Next, you *pay your vendors* . . . you pay the folks that give you credit.

After that, you *sell* the product to the customer, then *ship* the product to the customer.

After shipping, you wait a while to *collect from the customer.*

If we drew it as a diagram, it would look like this:

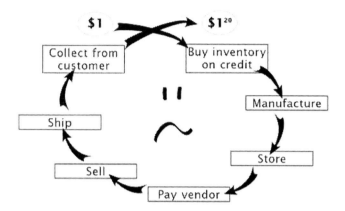

You put a dollar into the cycle at the beginning and you allow the dollar to work for you until the end, when you collect from the customer. Then chi-ching — 20 extra cents pops out . . . or 50 extra cents... or 49 extra dollars. What we are looking for here is an *extra*. This *extra* is your profit.

If you end the cycle and you have less than a dollar in your hand — say 90 cents — what you have is a *hobby*. And we don't like hobbies.

Notice the little wobbly smile on the diagram. That is because this is not the best application of our first principle. Let's look at who is using whose money.

When you purchase the inventory on credit , this does not affect your cash. We are fine so far. However, when you manufacture the product, it costs you to pay your people and run the factory. Storing it takes cash:

you have to pay to air-condition the facility, possibly hire guards, rent the facility, and so on.

Paying the vendor obviously consumes cash and selling the product or service does, too. When you sell, you have to pay for long distance telephone calls, travel, and possibly even commissions! Shipping consumes cash. And then, finally, at the end of the cycle, you get your money back when the customer pays you. So you are hemorrhaging cash until the very last moment of your sales cycle. This is not so good . . . you are using your own money.

How to Do It

NOW, if you could turn these events around, if you could change the sequence of each little step, what would you put first and what would you put last?

 Definitely, you would want to put paying the vendor last. And you will want to collect from the customer as early as possible.

Looking at a new diagram — a happy application of the first principle, — you will see that selling comes first. Then you create the product and ship it right out to the customer. After the customer receives it he is obligated to pay for it, and the very last step is paying the vendor.

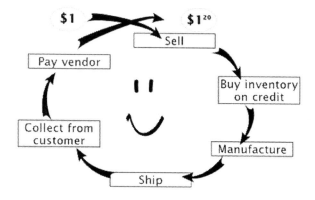

Notice that because you know exactly what the customer is going to buy and in what quantity, you don't have to store a bunch of finished goods in hopes that someone will buy it. Nice, huh?

Making Products Hoping Someone Will Buy Them Is Dangerous

In many industries, storing goods in hopes of selling them is dangerous. Things change so fast, you can't predict what the customer might want, and you might misfire on your estimates of what will sell. This is true in the computer industry for sure. New products are regularly coming out — and a manufacturer using the traditional method might get stuck with a bunch of inventory he doesn't want — and the customer doesn't want.

Dell Computer used to run their operation in the traditional fashion. Several of their main competitors, including Compaq, still do. Compaq sells its products in stores. This means they must hold a lot of inventory. They are making computers and hoping that someone will buy them.

Dell uses something they call the *direct method*, which means that they sell their product directly to the customer. There is no middleman.

Avoid Investing Your Time and Money in Products and Services You Aren't Sure Are Going to Sell

In my business, the speaking business, I will not develop a speech or a seminar until I have a commitment from someone to pay for it. I can conceptualize and outline the courses in order to entice the customer to buy them, but if they don't bite, I don't write. It doesn't make sense to me to develop a seminar that I am not sure anyone will buy. I don't want to have to force my clients to take on a seminar because I need to sell it.

I have met many speakers who develop a course, on — say — team leadership with some sort of unique twist, and try to sell it to customers. I find it is best, in terms of effort, to ask the customer what they want, and then see if I can meet their needs. This way it is customized for them and they feel special. I can add another seminar to my repertoire and everyone is happy.

This doesn't keep me from using a similar seminar or speech with other clients. As a matter of fact, some of my best seminars and speeches have come at the request of my clients and they sell over and over and over to a variety of folks.

Buying Products for Resale in Hopes Someone Will Buy Them Is Dangerous

Product manufacturers are interested in making their own sale. They will encourage their distributors and salesmen to buy products in advance or in bulk by offering incentives. Sometimes this technique is called packing the supply chain.

For instance, if you are a cosmetics salesperson — say a representative for Mary Kay or Avon — the mother company will ask you to buy a certain amount of product to use for demonstration. They may call it a sample box or a demo kit. They may offer you discounts for buying more product in advance than you need to fill current need.

 Be very careful about taking advantage of these offers or buying a super supreme sample box. It doesn't matter to the mother company if you move the stock out of your garage or not. The mother company has already made the sale — the sale to you.

When you end up with a closet full of product, you may have to discount it to move it. Maybe after it ages or expires, you will just have to throw it away.

The Three Phases of Business

There are three phases to a product's life — or a business cycle. The Four Principles of Happy Cash Flow™ and our subsequent discussion only apply to the SALES PHASE of a business.

The first phase is the INVESTMENT or DEVELOPMENT phase. For example, if you are a software company, you must spend time and resources developing and writing and testing the software.

The second phase of the business cycle is the SALES PHASE where you are actually making quantities of your product or service and selling it. For the software company, this is the phase where they print the software on a bunch of CDs, package it, and send it to a computer store to sell.

The third and last phase is the POST-SALE or CUSTOMER CARE PHASE. Some businesses have this phase, others do not. For the software developer, this would be where they answer customer calls or conduct training to help customers use the software.

So — again, our four principles only apply in the sales phase. We don't care, for now, about how much it costs to buy the equipment to run the company or how much debt they are in. This is just about the day-to-day business of cranking out cash.

Chapter 3:
The Second and Third Principles of Happy Cash Flow™

The second principle says that the fewer days you take to spin the cycle, the better. Shortening the number of days in the cycle ensures that you have maximum use of your own money and that others don't!

Again, let us compare and contrast. Let's say you are a homebuilder and it takes you half a year to build a home. So, it may take you 180 days to turn that cycle.

Contrast that to the number of days it takes to turn the cycle at Dell Computer. Their cycle turns several times a day — a thousand times a year. Based on just this principle, where would you rather your dollar be hanging out? Duh.

(The homebuilder is no dummy, of course. They make it on the fourth principle — see chapter 4.)

So the Second Principle
of Happy Cash Flow™ Is
Cut the Number
of Days in the Cycle

Metrics to Measure Your Success

There are three metrics that help us determine how many days it takes to turn the cycle: DSO, DSI, and DPO. These are great metrics for measuring how well you are managing cash. Let's talk about each one in turn.

DSO stands for *Days Sales Outstanding.* This measures the time it takes to collect from your customers. And we want this to be as little time as possible.

Looking at the cycle, DSO measures the number of days between the event of shipping and the event of collecting from the customer. In general, when we give credit, we allow our customers 30 days to pay. Some of our customers are going to pay much slower. (By the way, the method for calculating these metrics is included in the appendix to this book.)

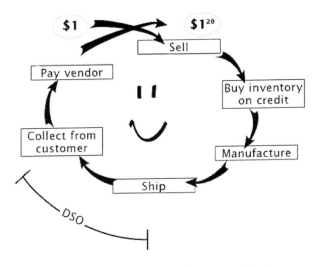

Now, Dell, as I told you earlier, wasn't always so smart. Prior to 1996 they used the traditional manufacturing model. Under this model their DSO number was 42. Now it is 34. That is a nice change.

What Can You Do to Collect from Customers Faster?

If you wanted to collect from your customers faster, what would you do? There is always your cousin Guido, the strong-arm, who is very persuasive when it comes to collecting. ☺

Other things you can do are:

- Hire more people to call customers to follow-up on late payments

- Use credit cards — credit cards pay in three days

- Invoice customers as quickly and accurately as possible

- Offer discounts for early payment

- Tighten credit policies — only allow customers who are likely to pay the opportunity to do business with you

> **Accounts Receivable Aging**
>
> Have you ever heard of the age of an accounts receivable? This is a similar concept to DSO. An aging of accounts receivables tells you how long each receivable has been outstanding. Usually, the collections department will compile a little spreadsheet that groups receivables into categories.
>
> Usually companies lump the amounts they are due from customers into groups of days. Some of their receivables are 30 or fewer days old, some are 31–45 days old, 46–60 days old, and then the dreaded over-60 days old. The customers showing up in the really old receivables list should be called, immediately.

 Think of Wal-Mart here. When I first started shopping at Wal-Mart, they would only take cash or check. No credit cards — because the three days it took them to collect on credit cards was too long.

Why Even Have Sales Outstanding at All?

Many businesses avoid outstanding sales altogether. They demand cash on delivery or, even better, demand cash in advance.

When you buy a bucket of chicken at KFC you pay for it right away — in cash. When you order a wedding gown, you pay the dress shop the entire amount up front — 18 weeks in advance of the delivery of the gown.

Would your customers accept such an arrangement? This way you have their money instead of them having your money. You never know until you ask. They may not mind at all.

The second metric is *DSI*. This stands for *Days Supply of Inventory*. This measures how many days worth of raw, in process, and finished goods inventory you have in stock. If you don't have inventory, I will give you an alternative measure later when we apply these principles to different industries.

Now, again, we want this number to be as short as possible. A large number may indicate that you are holding too much inventory in a phase of your manufacturing process.

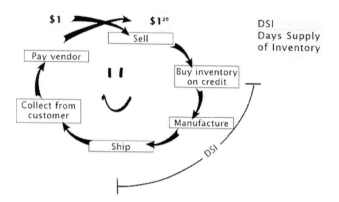

Dell has done an incredible job with this number. Before they implemented their "direct model" their DSI was 31 — in 2000 it was 6. Wow!

How Can You Reduce Your Inventory?

How can you do this, too?

- Change your sequence of events so that you only make what the customer wants — so you can ship it directly after manufacturing. No storage.

- Increase the speed of your manufacturing process so that you hold less.

- If you are a retailer, keep a close eye on the inventory items that move and don't move. The items that don't move can be returned to the vendor or sold at a discount to get them off the shelves.

An Innovative Way to Move Inventory

An owner of a small fabric store told me that keeping old inventory on her shelves was deadly, both to her cash flow and her customers' perceptions of her business. If items were dusty or outdated, her customers would eventually move on to her competitors who seemingly offered more trendy products.

To get a handle on her inventory, she implemented an inventory tracking software that gave her real-time information on items in her store. The software had the ability to generate reports that told her how long items had been on her shelves.

Her first action on old items was to move them to a more prominent location in her store, to attract more attention. If that didn't work, she would discount them. And if that didn't work, she would try to reformat the presentation of the item. For instance, she would cut the fabric off the bolts and present it in folded yard lengths or bundle together fabric, trim, and threads. She might also make a dress using the fabric and accessories to show how the items could be used.

She also created "mystery grab bags" full of items that didn't move, and sold them near the register. And if *that* didn't work, she would use the items as gifts to loyal customers. Whew, that's a lot of work.

The last metric is **DPO**. **DPO** stands for *Days Payables Outstanding*. This measures how long it takes to pay your suppliers. Now, we want this number to be long or big. A big number means that you hold on to your money for as long as you can.

Some businesses make the mistake of paying payables as soon as they get the bill in the mail. We will see in a moment why this is not the best practice.

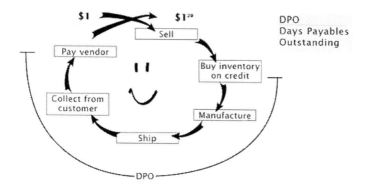

You can go overboard on this. Organizations that have clout and power can get tough with their vendors.

Dell negotiates with its vendors to pay in 45 days and then pays a little later. The standard length of time most businesses extend for credit purchases is 30 days.

Be Careful!!!

Be very careful when stretching payables. It can hurt other businesses. Sometimes, when I share this information I feel like I am putting good information in the wrong hands. I spoke once with a paper manufacturer who took these principles to heart. Their vendors are mom and pop logging operations in the Maine woods. Sounds quaint, doesn't it?

After my talk, I heard them say that they planned to stretch the payables to these loggers and that the loggers would have nothing to say about it. What could the mom and pops do? The paper manufacturer was their main customer.

If the paper manufacturer did end up implementing this plan, I am sure that some of the mom and pop logging operations are out of business now.

Dell's DPO in 1996 was near to standard at 33 days. In 2001, the number was 58. Quite an increase.

Dell is even considering raising the number to 80 days.

Why would a vendor put up with this? It is the vendor's cash at stake here. They are footing the bill and often have to get loans to finance the extra waiting time.

They put up with this because of volume. If you are a company that makes computer memory and Dell is the number one user of computer memory, you may decide you have to sell to Dell.

This does not mean you are getting the raw end of the deal as the vendor, but you do need to be careful to structure your relationship wisely. Here is an example of what not to do.

How *Not* to Structure Your Business Relationships

A woman I met in one of my workshops once had a company that made Christmas lights. Her company was based out of Louisiana and one of her specialties was manufacturing Cajun Christmas lights . . . lights with crawfish and jalapenos.

At the height of the Cajun craze, .
Wal-Mart approached her company
and asked her to put her product in
their stores. She was ecstatic. She
entered into an agreement with
Wal-Mart and went out to get a
loan to ramp up production. She
created enough lights to meet the
demand, and then shipped them out to Wal-Mart.

Unfortunately, the lights did not sell, and after the
season was over, Wal-Mart, under the terms of their
agreement, returned the lights to her company without
paying for them. Her company, of course, was unable
to make her loan payments and they went bankrupt.
Ehw! Not a pretty story.

What to Do Instead

What should she have done? Well, she could have
asked Wal-Mart to finance her increase in production.
Wal-Mart could have paid her up front so that she
could avoid going to a bank for financing.

She could have arranged for Wal-Mart to own the
inventory of Christmas lights and for them to be
obligated to pay her for them whether they sold or not.
She could have also asked for up-front payments for
the inventory from Wal-Mart for, let's say, a third of
her cost at the start of the contract, a third at delivery,
and then a third at the sale. This way, she would have
at least ended up with two-thirds of the money.

She could have planned for the possibility of the lights not selling at Wal-Mart and negotiated with another retailer to take them off her hands when and if they came back to her.

Use Credit Cards to Stretch Payments

One woman I know who owns a florist shop is a master at using other people's money without having a negative impact on her relationship with her vendors. She uses credit cards to do it.

She purchases her flowers and supplies from the vendor and waits for the vendor to bill her each month. The vendor allows her 30 days of credit. So on the 30th day, she calls the vendor and charges the payment on her credit card.

The credit card company bills her in 20 to 30 days for the purchase and she waits until the final day of the credit card cycle to pay her bill. She stretches the number of days in the cycle without bending any rules or making anyone do without their money. Of course, she uses credit cards to do it, but she feels it is worth it to keep her money for that long.

A More Equal Arrangement

As a vendor, you can insist on a more equal arrangement with your customers. For example a woman in one of my classes told me that she worked for a vitamin manufacturer and sold her vitamins through a major discount retail chain (which ended up going bankrupt in 2002).

This retailer, in an effort to keep up with Wal-Mart, sent her a letter, in a bland, small envelope, that stated that they were going to stretch the payment terms to her to 60 days and take a 10% discount on all future orders. It went on to say that her failure to respond to this letter would constitute her consent to these new conditions. Pretty tricky, huh?

Now this woman was smart. She knew that if she stood against this major retailer alone, they would tell her to take a walk, and they could buy their vitamins elsewhere. She wisely decided to call her competitors and asked them to stand with her to resist these new policies.

Some of her competitors had lost or ignored the letter because it looked so innocuous and were very happy to hear from her. They stood against the retailer and "won" — won to keep the status quo.

We will cover other arrangements and businesses later.

How the Metrics Add Up

Now that we have the three metrics defined, we need to add them up.

> ## DSO + DSI – DPO =
> ## Total Number of Days
> ## in the Cash Conversion Cycle

This number indicates how long it takes a company to turn an investment of $1 into $1 plus a little profit. Another way to say it is that it counts the number of days in the cycle of converting cash into more cash, hence the title *cash conversion cycle.*

How Many Days Does It Take to Turn Cash into More Cash?		Dell 1996	Dell 2000
add	DSO – Days Sales Outstanding	42	34
plus	DSI – Days Supply of Inventory	31	6
less	DPO – Days Payables Outstanding	33	58
equals	Total Number of Days in the Cash Conversion Cycle	+40	-18

Wow, this number for Dell went from a positive 40 in 1996 to negative 18 in 2001. Quite a difference! So what does that mean?

Consider what a positive number "1" would mean. It would mean that the company would have to keep one day's worth of cash on hand at all times and that the sales cycle turns once a day or 360 times a year. So 360 times a year it cranks out its 20-cent profit. Then what would positive 40 mean?

That means that the company would need 40 days of cash on hand and the cycle would spin around nine times a year. Only nine times would you get your profit out the back end of the process.

And you know what? That is about average. 30 to 40 days is a "normal" sales cycle.

 Now what does negative 18 mean? Yep, it means that Dell has other people's money for 18 days. It means that the cycle spins several times a day, hundreds of times a year. It means that Dell *never* has to reach into its own pocket for cash. Pretty sweet, right?

What does Dell do with all this extra cash? It invests it. So in addition to making profits from selling computers, Dell also makes profits from investing its billions of dollars of extra cash. It also uses the extra cash to grow and to run the business on a day-to-day basis.

Little Things Can Add Days to Your Cash Conversion Cycle

Simple things like how fast you bill, how fast the mail runs, how promptly and how often you deposit your receipts, how promptly the bank will give you use of your deposits, and how long it takes your payments to reach and be deposited by your vendors can affect the length of your cash conversion cycle.

Some businesses use electronic funds transfers and lockboxes in order to get their money faster. Some pay their vendors from remote locations, by check, so that their money isn't available to the vendor. These tricks are often called "playing the float."

Shaving or adding a day here or there can impact your cash flow needs significantly.

For instance, let's say you are a consultant and that you bill your clients every month. So you may have already accumulated 30 days of work before you bill. It may take three days for the bill to get to the client in the mail, and if they are nice they pay in 30 days. It takes three more days to get to you, two days for you to get to the bank, and then the bank holds your funds, to make sure they clear, for four more days. We are now up to 69 days. This means you could work on January 1 and not see the money until the middle of March. Aargh! How are you going to pay your rent at that rate?

One solution here is to bill more often . . . say weekly. Another is to fax or email your bills. Another is to accept electronic payment. You can also negotiate with your bank, or shop around for a bank that doesn't hold on to your funds for so long. All worth working on so that you do not have to go get a loan – and pay interest – just to operate on a day-to-day basis.

This leads us to the third principle:

The Third Principle of Happy Cash Flow™ Is
Pump Up the Volume

Now that we reduced the number of days in the cycle, we need to spin the cycle as frequently as possible. We need velocity! We need to increase the number of transactions. Because every time it spins, chi-ching — 20 cents pops out. YEAH! More profit for us!

Even a homebuilder can use this principle. Even though it takes 180 days to spin the cycle, he can build tens or even hundreds of homes a year. And each time a house closes, he collects profit.

Think of Dell and Wal-Mart. Talk about huge numbers of transactions!

 And every time Dell increases market share, as Dell becomes a larger sales organization, as Dell grows as it did over the 1996 to 2000 period from a $5 billion dollar to a $25 billion dollar company — each day of other people's money it holds is bigger.

Wow, if only we could all have billions of extra cash. Sigh.

Think of the reverse situation. If Dell had allowed other people to use its money, had kept its cash conversion cycle at a positive 40 days while increasing the number of transactions in its business, it would have needed an enormous amount of cash from loans or other sources to run its business.

So we have seen how Dell does a nice job with using other people's money, cutting the number of days in the cycle, and velocity, now we need to look at where Dell has a bit of a challenge — in principle number four.

The Four Principles of Happy Cash Flow™

Chapter 4:
The Fourth Principle
of Happy Cash Flow™

The happiest business in the world is one where you put a little bit of money in and get a lot out of the back end. In our earlier example, we would like the sales cycle to generate more than 20 cents for our investment. Wouldn't it be great if we could get 80 cents out? How about $3? Even better!

The basic formula of profit is REVENUES less EXPENSES equals PROFIT. So in order to raise profit, you have to either increase revenues or decrease expenses . . . or both.

**The Fourth Principle
of Happy Cash Flow™ Is
Put a Little In, Get a Lot Out**

Companies that operate in a competitive environment are often hard pressed to increase profits. In a competitive environment, you can't charge whatever you like for your product or service. The market dictates the cap, the upper limit of price. Even worse, if the market terms your product a "commodity," you are in even more of a cash squeeze. A commodity means everyone has one or can get one, so no one wants to pay much for your product.

Dell cannot charge more for its computers than its competitors and Wal-Mart can't charge more than Kmart or Target. And the cost of creating the product or service is likely increasing. If, as happened in 1998, the selling price of a laptop decreased while the cost of memory increased, the profit margin that Dell made per product got squeezed. This is not a good thing.

Luckily, all is not lost because commodity companies can implement the McDonald's "Want fries with that?" concept.

The McDonald's "Want Fries with That?" Concept

Every time you walk into a McDonald's and order something, they ask you, "Do you want fries with that?" "Would you like to super-size it?"

Why do they push the fries and bucket-sized soft drinks so hard? Because each of those products has a *huge* profit margin. Fries don't cost much to make per bag and soft drinks are incredibly cheap.

And the beautiful thing, from McDonald's perspective, is that we don't even pay attention to the cost of the fries. They could raise the price on us indefinitely . . . OK, if they were $2 a bag, we might say something, but they do have some flexibility here.

And the soft drinks are so cheap it costs more in labor to fill and refill your drink . . . so now they let you fill the bucket yourself.

The burger is the commodity. They have to keep that product competitively priced to match Burger King and Jack in the Box. If they raise their price too much, we may balk and walk over to the competitor.

But take something like the McFlurry, which is their ice-cream desert. That thing sells for $1.50 or more! It can't cost anywhere near that to make. It is milk, and sugar, and crumbled cookies. Come on!

Remember when McDonald's wouldn't even consider customizing your burger? I am a "pickles and ketchup only" kind of girl. I had to wait for 30 minutes when I was a kid to get my burger. It totally threw them off. They couldn't afford to spend more time on the burger because they weren't making much of a profit on it. Competitive pressure caused them to change their processes to give us a customized burger, like Burger King did and does.

Now they have started packaging the meal all together in a bundle — the fries, the soft drink, and the burger — and calling it a Super Value Meal. Is it such a value? A "Super Value"? We don't know, and we don't care. No one stands there and adds it up on a calculator. We trust them. What marketing genius! Now we have no idea how much the individual components cost.

Have you ever been "super-sized" in an electronics store? Recently I purchased a DVD player at a large electronic appliance retailer. Yes, the price of the unit was cheap, but the accessories, warranty, and service agreement added substantially to the cost by the time I checked out.

Defining Profit Margin

You have probably heard the term "profit margin" many times and possibly even applied to different items. This is because there are several categories of profit margin.

All the word margin means is remainder. It is the result of subtracting something from something else. We want to minimize the amount of money we put into the product or service and maximize the selling price.

Looking at the income statement you see the basic formula of income or profit is Revenues – Expenses = Profit.

For management purposes, a company usually does some sub-totals inside the income statement.

If you take total sales and subtract cost of goods sold you end up with GROSS PROFIT MARGIN. If you subtract operating expenses from gross profit margin, you get OPERATING PROFIT MARGIN. If you subtract other expenses, such as taxes, you get NET PROFIT MARGIN. This is the final subtotal.

The Four Principles of Happy Cash Flow™

1. Use Other People's Money

In other words, make sure to pay your payables late, keep inventory low, and get your money from your customers as fast as possible.

2. Cut the Number of Days

Here, you want to cut the number of days that your money is tied up unnecessarily in receivables and inventory, and increase the number of days you hold on to your money in the form of payables. We covered three metrics to measure the number of days in the cycle — DSO, DSI, and DPO.

3. Pump Up the Volume

The more transactions you run through your now efficient cash conversion cycle, the better.

4. Put a Little In, Get a Lot Out

Increase your profit margins by selling at the maximum price and spending as little as possible to create your product or service. You may have to apply the McDonald's "Want fries with that?" concept to keep margins high overall.

Chapter 5:
Who Else Is
Doing It Right?

So who else is doing it right?

The quick and easy answers would be Southwest Airlines and Wal-Mart.

Southwest Airlines

What is Southwest Airlines' philosophy? "Get as many people on a plane as cheaply as possible as fast as possible." Cut prices and gain market share. After the September 11 attacks, they were the financially healthiest airline — with *$1 billion* in cash in reserve. This allowed them to survive the slowdown that crushed other airlines. The COO states that even in the best of times they run the airline as if they were the worst of times.

Think of how it
works on Southwest
Airlines. They don't
serve food, just little

bags of peanuts and snacks. They charge for alcohol
and don't have a first class with unlimited food and
alcohol. Instead of issuing paper boarding passes they
use the same plastic set of boarding cards every flight.

They pack us on the plane and make only short trips. If
you want to fly from Austin to Ft. Lauderdale for
instance, as I did once, it means stopping four times
along the way. They often operate out of the
"alternative" airport in a major city, thereby saving on
landing and departure fees . . . and on and on and on.

Southwest Airlines makes no attempt to be the airline
that will meet all your needs and fly wherever you
want to go. If the route is not profitable, Southwest
will not fly it.

Flying Southwest Airlines is far from a luxury
experience, but they can be counted on to offer the
least expensive fares and drive the competition in cities
where they operate to do the same. All these cost-
saving measures are a good application of Principle
Number Four, "Put a Little In, Get a Lot Out" — I
would say.

Wal-Mart

Wal-Mart. No discussion of current business is complete without looking at Wal-Mart.

 The inventory you see on Wal-Mart's shelves doesn't really belong to Wal-Mart. In essence, inventory is handled on a consignment basis. With 4500 stores in the US, they have substantial clout with their vendors.

Let's say you sell potholders to Wal-Mart. Wal-Mart asks you, the vendor, to tell them how many potholders will sell in each location. You are responsible for coordinating shipments to make sure the potholders get in their distribution centers and then onto the stores. You may even end up stocking the shelves.

If the potholder sells, Wal-Mart pays you in 60+ days. If the potholder doesn't sell, Wal-Mart sends it back to you and charges you a penalty for taking up shelf space. You, of course, don't get paid for the potholder. This is, essentially, a consignment situation.

Zara Fashions

Clothing retailers often get stuck with merchandise that doesn't sell, leaving them with high amounts of inventory . . . oftentimes in the wrong season to sell it.

This high amount of inventory has even spawned other retailers to handle the excess, such as TJ Maxx, Marshall's, and Ross Dress for Less . . . but that is another subject.

A Spanish company, called Zara, has figured out a way to avoid high inventory balances. Zara manufactures its own clothing in local sewing shops and makes a minimal quantity of each item. If the item flies off the racks, Zara makes more. If not, they move on to the next item.

This fast turnaround arrangement makes Zara very appealing to its young fashion-conscious customers. As soon as a new style becomes hot, Zara can put it on their shelves. Outdated merchandise doesn't stay on the rack long.

Free Checking?

Have you noticed lately how many banks are offering free checking? Do you think they are doing this out of the goodness of their hearts or because competition from credit unions is forcing them to? Think again.

Banks make more money on free checking accounts. Two of our four principles are at work here — Principle Number Three, "Pump Up the Volume" and Principle Number Four, — "Put a Little In, Get a Lot Out."

First: volume. Free checking attracts more customers than checking accounts that charge fees.

Next: customers that are attracted to free checking accounts may not have the requisite "minimum balances" that banks require on regular checking accounts. This is actually a plus for banks because they are limited by law on the amount of fees they can charge for not meeting a minimum balance but they are not limited on the amount they can charge for a bounced check.

It turns out that many of the customers attracted to free checking also end up bouncing checks because they do not keep enough money in their account. The bank ends up making much more off of these customers than if it charged them for checking. This is the principle of putting a little in and getting a whole lot out.

Chapter 6:
A Look at Other Businesses

Let's run through a few other businesses that we are all familiar with and get an understanding of how they apply the principles. Remember, most companies do not do all four principles well. They excel in one or two or do fair to middling in all.

If you are doing well in all four, congratulations. AND don't expect it to last forever! Because if your business is kicking, making money hand over fist, someone else is always watching, and they may decide to go into your business also.

As soon as that happens, you are in a competitive situation, which usually ruins Principle Number Four, "Put a Little In, Get a Lot Out."

So to recap: first, use other people's money by collecting as soon as possible, holding a very small inventory (or no inventory) and stretching payables. Second, shave as many days as you can off the total number of days in the cash conversion cycle. Once you have this set up, then work to increase the volume of transactions running through your business. And lastly, cut costs and increase the selling price of your products and services. Consider creating high-margin products, services, or add-ons ("fries") and enticing your customers to buy them.

 There are very few industries that have maintained their dominance for more than a decade. A long time ago, railroads were the tops. Then it was steel, then cars, then aerospace, and then computers. If you figure out who is next, please call me.

So the Big Boys Can Do This, But Can I?

Oh, yes. You don't have to be big in order to be smart about how you manage your cash.

Remember the story of the florist who used credit cards to manage her payables.

Most graphic artists get 1/3 of their fee up front, 1/3 after acceptance of concept, and 1/3 at delivery of the work. They also get a commission from the printer. This is standard practice in the advertising and graphics industry, meaning that they are never using their own money to operate.

Several tax accountants I know demand payment for preparing a tax return up front. If they end up spending more time preparing the return than they expected, they charge the remainder before they will deliver the completed return.

Many of my colleagues — professional speakers — demand their fee for speaking when the "gig" is booked, not the date the gig is performed. This can mean that they have the cash in hand months before they have to perform.

It Won't Work in My Industry!

I'm not buying that! Even if it is standard practice in your industry to do things one way, that doesn't mean you have to. Back to the tax accountants, industry standard says that they get their money when billing the client *after* the return is prepared. Can you imagine how many of those "standard practice" accountants get stiffed every year?

And you can be niche-y and smarter than the average bear. Zara is in the retail clothing business, yet they do not operate like everyone else. Dell and Wal-Mart do not operate like the others in their industries, and thus are thriving.

Two Different Philosophies in the Same Industry

To a consumer, a hardware store is a hardware store is a hardware store when you need a hammer or a plunger, a key or a wrench.

But in Austin, we have several different kinds of hardware stores, each successful because of a unique implementation of the four principles. You are probably familiar with the huge hardware retailer, Home Depot. We have several of those in Austin. And we also have a specialty hardware store called Breed and Co.

Breed and Co. is a fun place to shop. On one side of the store, you have a small hardware store with very attentive and experienced clerks who can answer just about any hardware or home repair question. Most of the clerks are over 50 years old. They know what they are doing.

On the other side of the store is a garden center, a gourmet chocolate shop, and an upscale kitchen goodies store. I registered for my wedding at Breed and Co. because they had such unique and beautiful things.

Breed and Co. is not known for its sales or its low prices on hardware. And because their hardware store is so small, they may not have just what you need.

Contrast this with Home Depot. Home Depot will likely have what you need, even if it is some odd-sized nail, because they carry a whole aisle of nails. And Home Depot is going to provide the nail at a low cost. Home Depot has great products, but whatever you buy there, everyone may already have — they are on the tail end of home décor trends.

And the big thing you sometimes can't get at Home Depot is experienced help, help that will spend the time with you to help figure out a home repair problem.

So, if you really need expert help, you would be wise to visit Breed and Co. and possibly pay a little more for your goodies. If you are concerned about cost and know what you are looking for and want to only go to one place to get it, Home Depot is your place.

Home Depot makes it by "pumping up the volume." Breed and Co. makes it on "put a little in, get a lot out."

A Pizza Franchise

Please keep in mind that these principles only apply when looking at the sales phase of a business. The sales phase, in this case, is when you are cranking out the pizzas. Pizza! Pizza! Pizza! We don't care, right now, about how much it cost to buy the franchise or the equipment.

So, do they apply principle number one? Do they "Use Other People's Money?"

YES, they do. Customers pay for the pizza in cash the second it arrives at their door. Pizza Shack does not send you a statement every month

with a big pig stamped on it telling you that you ate five cheese pizzas over the past three weeks. Thank goodness our gluttony is not documented that plainly.

And, they do pay for their supplies later. They pay for the sauce, dough, and other goodies after they receive the cash. In the restaurant business, they pay faster than the standard 30 days because food is perishable . . . but we can assume that they are doing fine with the first two principles.

Success with the third principle, "Pump Up the Volume," depends on how fabulous a neighborhood they are located in. If it is a neighborhood full of working parents, children, teenagers, and the occasional glutton (me!) they are going to do fine. Pizza! Pizza! Pizza!

But, principle number four is where they have their problem. Competition puts a cap on the amount they can charge for their pizzas — and making and delivering pizzas isn't so cheap. As a matter of fact, pizza makers carefully weigh the amount of cheese they put on each pizza and count the number of pepperoni!

Now, they have "fries" also. Think of those silly breadsticks. Those can't cost much to make. And chicken wings or hot wings. Chicken processors used to pay to have the chicken wings taken away. Now they are all the rage. Drinks, beer, salads . . . I would imagine these are "fries", and we do not, as consumers, require them to competitively price these things.

Sometimes, as in the case of Domino's and those tasty Cinnasticks, they apply the drug dealer's tactics. They give the Cinnasticks to us free at first and when we are hooked, start charging! Cinnasticks, crack . . . same principle.

A Trade-Off Between the Principles

As I mentioned in the first chapter, you can do well on some of these principles, but usually not all. And every business decision involves a tradeoff between the principles. You may have to sacrifice one to improve the other.

Now, let's say you are a successful little Pizza Shack. You have a loyal client base and life is good. But, unfortunately, a competitor — Cheesy's Maximum Pizza — has moved in down the block. You are losing customers fast. Everyone wants to try Cheesy's and Cheesy's pizzas are good — just as good as yours.

EECK! What do you do? Your volume has slowed considerably. To pump up volume, you could send out a coupon to bring your customers back. Of course, this messes with the fourth principle, "Put a Little In, Get a Lot Out," because you are cutting your selling price and reducing your margins.

After a few months, you notice that you are not bringing in the cash or the profits that you were. So you decide to cut costs. You put less cheese on the pizza, you hire cheaper (and more snarly) delivery kids, and you put fewer wings in the hot wing bucket. OOOOH NO — not a good idea.

The loyal customers you did hold onto initially quit you.

What is an alternative to this ugly scenario? **Differentiation.** Somehow your customers have to believe that your product is **better** than Cheesy's — that you are worth the extra cost. You could use higher quality ingredients, appeal to children somehow, make yourself "cool" by marketing to teens, get involved more in your community, or, like Pizza Hut, offer a dazzling array of products — cheese-stuffed crust, NY crust, thin and crispy crust, etc.

It is going to be a long, but worthwhile, battle. Welcome to capitalism.

A Service Model, a Contingency Lawyer

Let's go to the other extreme, a service not a product model. Let's say you are a lawyer working on contingency. You don't get your money unless you win your case.

This is a very precarious cash flow situation indeed. I once met a banker whose primary clients were lawyers working on contingency who needed loans until their case was won.

Consider the lawyers who argued the tobacco cases. Do they use other people's money? Definitely not.

They must invest their own time and effort, the time and effort of their staff, and their office expenses to be able to finance the battle.

I have a friend whose son suffers from brain damage, likely caused by the obstetrician during birth. She went to many lawyers asking them to take her case. Because it was not a cut-and-dried, for-sure win, no one would take her case. One lawyer offered to take it on if she had $50,000 to contribute first. Since her son was taking so much extra care and cash, in no way could she come up with that money.

She was so angry, but it was unrealistic of her to expect that these lawyers should take her case out of the goodness of their hearts. They also have families to support.

The lawyer is a bit of a high stakes gambler. They can't take on possible loser cases because they don't have extra time or extra resources.

They don't have volume and their cash conversion cycle takes forever. It can sometimes take years to win the case.

But, oh, the last principle. Yes, it appears that lawyers make mucho bucks. But given this crazy cash flow situation, they have to have it to survive.

How do lawyers get around this? Sometimes they ask for retainers. Sometimes they get their money up front. Sometimes they save money from the previous case to last them a while, get interim financing, or use their favorite cash flow management tactic . . . band together in packs. Excuse me, I mean *firms*. (Hey, I couldn't resist.) This way *someone's* money is coming in *some*time. It is how they pump up the volume. The corporate lawyer, the tax lawyer, the personal injury lawyer . . . all together with different timings on their cash conversion cycle — that is one reason why law firms are so big.

A Multi-Level Marketer

Multi-level marketers make a profit in two ways — from selling a product and from taking a percentage of what their affiliates sell farther down the line.

For example, when the front-line salesperson sells a bottle of vitamins to a customer, they collect 100% of the retail price from the customer. The front-line salesperson keeps 25%, pays 50% for the product, and pays another 25% to the person that brought them into the program.

The person that brought them into the program turns around and pays the person that brought them into the program 25% of their cut and so on and so on up the chain. Someone who has several levels of salespeople and supervisors — or affiliates — underneath them could, conceptually, never sell a product directly to a customer, but still be bringing in income.

If a multi-level marketer works things just right, she can apply all Four Principles of Happy Cash Flow™.

If she asks customers to pay her before she calls her distributor to order the product, she doesn't use her own money or get stuck with excess inventory. So she is doing well on Principle Number One — "Use Other People's Money" and Principle Number Two — "Cut the Number of Days in the Cycle."

If she has a large clientele, she can keep the volume flowing. If she can elicit someone to sell on her behalf — if she becomes a supervisor — then she can benefit from the volume created by others' efforts. So, she is doing well on Principle Number Three — "Pump Up the Volume."

And the margins on these products are generous. Generous enough for her to share a cut with her supervisor and several people up the chain of command. So the potential is there to make it on Principle Number Four — "Put a Little In, Get a Lot Out." And I say POTENTIAL because the product is not the only cost of doing business.

She must also advertise, pay for office supplies, telephone, gas, Internet access, possibly rent . . . and the list goes on and is unique to each salesperson's approach to her business. If too much money is spent "running" the business, then the profit made on each product evaporates. As with any business, the danger of turning into one of those hobbies I mentioned in the first chapter is there.

A Not-for-Profit

A not-for-profit also has to worry about cash flow. They need cash to support their operations and pay their staff and provide services.

What often messes up their cash flow is grants — grants that fund on the reimbursement basis. Many federal grants require that a grantor spend the money first, accumulate the costs, and then seek reimbursement monthly. Then the federal government takes a month to reimburse the grantee.

This is a cash flow mess. If the not-for-profit wants the money, they have to put up with this? Well, maybe not. The feds have been known to be reasonable.

They may be willing to reimburse on a weekly or even daily basis. They may give you some costs up front and ask you to justify the rest. It doesn't have to be this way.

Of course, billing on a daily basis takes time, but can help ensure you don't run out of cash as often.

Instead of DSI — Days Supply of Inventory — the metric you would be concerned with is *Days Between Billings*. The longer you wait, the longer your cash conversion cycle will take.

Some not-for-profits choose to reject grants that have such bad cash flow effects and are paperwork intensive. They prefer direct gifts and donations, if they can get them. You can also renegotiate with a grantor to change the sequence of events.

.

Chapter 7:
What to Do Now

Now that you understand what makes cash flow FLOW — it is time to examine your own business, possibly make a few changes, and monitor the results of your efforts.

Here are some questions designed to help you find that extra cash:

1. Do you use other people's money?

    a. Do you allow your customers to pay you after you deliver your product or service?

        i. Can you ask your customers to pay you in full or in part up front or on delivery?

        ii. Can you speed collections?

b. Do you hold a large inventory?

    i. Can you reduce the amount of inventory you hold?

    ii. Can you modify the expectation of your customers so that you do not have to have everything they want immediately? Can they wait a few days for you to order it and ship it to them?

c. Do you take a long time to bill clients?

d. Do you pay your payables immediately?

2. How can you increase your volume?

3. How can you increase your margins?

a. Can you raise prices or cut costs?

b. Can you apply the McDonald's "Want fries with that?" concept

c. Can you eliminate your less profitable customers?

A list of ideas for reducing receivables, reducing inventory, and stretching payables follows in Chapters 8, 9, and 10.

Chapter 8:
Ideas for
Minimizing Inventory

Let's turn our attention first to inventory. In general, you would prefer to minimize inventory because if your resources are tied up in inventory, they aren't available to respond to business opportunities, or even do simple things like cover payroll and bills.

Here are a variety of ways to help you reduce the amount of inventory you currently hold. Some of these will not apply to you directly, but may get you thinking about some other innovative way to manage your inventory.

Make the vendor keep the inventory

Is there a way your suppliers can keep the inventory on hand at their warehouses instead of you purchasing it and putting it in your warehouse? This will reduce the need for storage space and will also save you from holding unwanted items that are no longer selling.

Have vendors ship the inventory to customers

Amazon.com's initial business plan eliminated the need to hold inventory. When a customer ordered a book on line, that order would be forwarded to the publisher of the book through the Amazon website. Amazon got a cut of the sale but never had to touch the inventory. But because some publishers had poor systems for shipping orders, customers were waiting far too long for their product. Amazon had to buy the inventory and ship it themselves. This tied up their cash and their profitability suffered accordingly. Now eBay, on the other hand, is an ideal Internet business. eBay is just a conduit for people to trade goods. They get a cut of every sale without having to make an investment in the inventory.

Outsource components

Is there a piece of your product or service that you could splinter off or give to someone else? For instance, let's say you are a restaurant and you offer desserts. Instead of baking the desserts yourself, you could order desserts from a baker and have them delivered to you daily. If you are a retailer you can sublet sections of your store. Several department stores in my area do not run or own their shoe departments. Instead, they lease the space to a company that just specializes in shoes.

Order inventory just-in-time

Here you order only what you need when you need it. In this scenario, the only inventory you hold is inventory-in-process. Dell Computer Corporation uses this method. The only inventory they hold is components in process of being manufactured or finished computers waiting to be shipped to the customer.

Pay only as you use the inventory

This is how Wal-Mart plays the game. Let's say you sell potholders to Wal-Mart. If your potholder sells, Wal-Mart pays you in 60+ days. If your potholder doesn't move quickly off the shelves, they start marking down prices on your product. You've seen the little smiley face Zorro knocking cents off the prices. Well, Wal-Mart doesn't pay for those discounts, the vendor does. If your potholder still doesn't sell, ever, Wal-Mart returns the potholder to you and charges you a penalty for taking up shelf space. Wal-Mart is essentially a warehouse to put your inventory in. Would some of your vendors accept that arrangement? Would they be willing to give you inventory on consignment in hopes that your customers will buy it?

Vending machine

Aircraft mechanics need a wide variety of parts and need them fast. To satisfy this need, parts vendors set up vending machines in the hangers. When the mechanics need a part, they punch in a code and out the part pops. The airline only pays for parts it uses and it is the responsibility of the vendor to keep the vending machines well stocked. Only after the item is requested is it charged to the mechanic.

Order in real time

Once an order is entered into a computer it can trigger a purchase from a vendor. You don't have to take any extra steps to have the items delivered; the computer program automatically makes the order. This speeds the service to the customer and ensures that only needed items are delivered

Use Kaizen/six sigma principles to garner efficiencies

Kaizen and six-sigma are popular philosophies regarding quality. Both argue that you can always find efficiencies in your processes. These efficiencies will save you money and time. In a service business, the principles direct you to shorten the time between when the service is ordered and when it is delivered and billed. If you are a manufacturer, the principles direct you to shorten the time that you spend in the manufacturing process. This means that you spend less time holding work in process inventory.

Improve the quality of your product or service

Low quality products and services need replacement and repair. And replacement and repair takes extra inventory. Look to the principles of Kaizen and Total Quality Management for inspiration.

Reward employees

Educate employees about your goal to reduce inventory and then give them an incentive for making it happen. Count the amount of inventory you have on hand today and set targets for reducing it. Measure and communicate your progress frequently. What gets measured gets done.

Make products *to order* instead of *to sell*

Instead of manufacturing items hoping to sell them, make only what you know the customer wants and is obligated to pay for. This is the way that Gateway Computer does business. The customer walks into one of their demo stores and selects a computer. But the customer does not walk out with the computer. It is shipped to them a few days later. This is a different approach to inventory than a computer company that sells its products in an electronics store, say Best Buy. In this case, the computer manufacturer must predict ahead of time what they think will sell. If technology changes or customers do not want the product, the store and the computer manufacturer end up holding excess inventory and may have to discount it to move it.

Allow only limited access to inventory

Fraud investigators say that fraud starts with opportunity. If a person is given opportunity to steal, the temptation may be too strong for them to resist. If your employees, contractors, or customers have unreasonable access, you should consider ways to limit or control their access.

Sell by-products of the manufacturing process.

Instead of throwing away waste, sell it. For example, wine makers sell the casks that their wine is fermented in. Marble quarries sell the rubble left after mining the large blocks.

Use the same inventory items to create multiple products

This is the Taco Bell tactic. If you think about it, Taco Bell has only a few inventory items on hand — they just use them to create multiple products. For instance, the ground beef appears in tacos, chalupas, nachos, burritos, and salads. The flour tortillas wrap burritos, tacos, and are used for quesadillas.

Reduce models and options

This has been a big time-saver of time for my business. I make a better living if I do not totally rewrite my courses each time I teach them. If I can wake up in the morning and get right into a class that I have taught multiple times to a similar audience, I am doing well. There are several topics I refuse to teach because it will take too much of my time to develop the topic. You cannot be everything to every customer. Niche and specialize to reduce your inventory.

Stock only items that have a quick turnaround

For this to work, you must keep a close eye on what sells and what doesn't. This may require you to purchase and use inventory-tracking software. Items that do not sell should not be stocked. The customer can be promised they will receive the items in a few weeks.

Manage customer expectations

If the customer does not expect to leave your store with the item, then you can just hold samples. How wonderful that would be! For instance, most bridal shops take the bride's full payment for the dress and deliver 18 weeks later. And when it arrives, it doesn't even fit! It has to be altered, which takes another month. You may think that having inventory on hand is an important component of customer satisfaction — but have you asked? Maybe the customer doesn't really care about being able to walk home with it. Maybe they value selection and payment options more.

Tear down the warehouse

My clothes expand to fill my closet. My books expand to fill my bookshelves, and so on. The same could be said of business inventory. If you get rid of the warehouse, you will have to liquidate what you currently have and be extremely careful about what you purchase in the future.

Evaluate clients

Let's face it, some customers are pains! Usually, 20% of your customers cause 80% of your headaches. Every year you should sit down and evaluate who you are doing business with. Maybe the customer who demands the most and pays the least is sucking up all your time and causing you to hold extra inventories. It's time to wean yourself off their business and make room for the new.

Get rid of obsolete inventory

Do something to get rid of obsolete inventory. Liquidate it. Give it away, if necessary. If it is large stuff, it is taking up space and costing you money to maintain. If you are a retailer, dusty inventory on your shelves looks tacky and unappealing to customers. Get any money you can out of it and move on . . . and try not to buy too much stuff again.

Increase the accuracy of your inventory forecasts

The better you know your sales cycles, the less inventory you will have to hold. Perhaps you always sell more around the holidays or at the beginning of a year? I met one man who was the CFO for a grocery chain in Colorado. He said that he budgeted daily for each store. He had four staff running the numbers. He tracked how many inventory items were selling at each store and predicted their needs for the coming few days. He knew what time the customers shopped each day and what their buying behavior was around holidays and special events. If he got one too many shipments of perishable foods, it might eat up his profit.

Limit returns

Do not allow the customer an unlimited time to return an item. Lands' End — a clothing retailer — allows returns until the end of time. No matter when your item breaks, you are allowed to return it. I once returned a pair of jeans specially manufactured for me in tall size 12 after three years because the zipper busted. I faulted the manufacture of the jeans, when it was really my fat rear end that caused the breakage.

I was so deep in denial, I didn't think of what the salesperson was doing by offering me a larger size. This means they now have a useless pair of jeans as well as sending me a new replacement pair of jeans in a size 14. Initiate a policy that allows the customers to return unused items only with a receipt within seven days. This way you are not in danger of getting your materials back after they have become obsolete. Document your policy on receipts and invoices. Otherwise you could end up with stuff you don't want months or maybe years down the line.

Reduce try-before-you-buy and rental programs

If you allow customers to try it before they buy it you must have items on hand to both sell to try out. This might in essence, double your inventory. If you use a rental program, the products will eventually come back. Evaluate the benefits of the revenue stream vs. what happens when you get old inventory back. What are you going to do with the used inventory then? Sell it for scrap? Dispose of it entirely? Use it yourself? Rent it to the next guy? What does all this cost?

Chapter 9:
Ideas for Collecting Faster

Remember Wimpy saying to Popeye, "I will gladly pay you Tuesday for a hamburger today!"? Do you think Wimpy ever paid up?

If you grant your customers credit, you are letting them use your resources — eat your burgers — for a time without having to pay you for it. They have the benefit of your product or service while you wait to get the cash you need to pay your bills.

It is always in your best interest to get your customers to pay you as quickly as possible.

Here are some ideas for collecting from your customers faster:

Bill on the Internet

Can you encourage your customers to pay you over the Internet using credit cards, PayPal, or a similar service? This way, they may pay your bill as soon as they receive it.

Get deposits from customers

If you have customers you suspect might never pay you, ask for a deposit. If they do not return your item or wait too long to pay, you can use their deposit to pay for the product and your effort.

Use milestone billing for long-term projects

This holds for both services and for manufacturing. One company I know of makes very specialized medical equipment averaging over $100,000 retail. Each custom piece of equipment takes them up to three months to manufacture. Instead of waiting until the product is shipped to bill — which might stretch their investment in the product up to half a year — three months to build and three months to wait on payments from slow-paying hospitals — the company charges 50% for the item up front, 25% on shipment, and 25% on terms. This is much easier on their cash flow.

Automatically debit customer's accounts

Can you establish an ongoing relationship that makes monthly payments necessary? Can you justify withdrawing the payments directly from their bank account or charging their credit card? This is how tanning salons make their business work. In the north, most people do not tan in the winter. So, at most, the tanning salon would have an "on" season for six months out of the year.

Where do they get cash to operate for the rest of the year? Savvy tanning salons sell the client a tanning package that allows them to tan a limited number of times each month for the entire year. Even though the customer does not tan in December, the salon still gets a bit of cash flow.

Health clubs are similar. I finally canceled my health club membership after not going for ten months. I paid $45 a month for those ten months and never used the facility. I didn't want to cancel because of my hope of going AND the hefty re-registration fee if I wanted to start with them again. They have $450 of my money and didn't have to provide me with any service.

Negotiate with your bank
to make your money available sooner

Some banks will hold any checks they receive for deposit for three to five days before they will make the funds available for use by the depositor. There is not some sort of federal law that requires them to do this; this is the bank's choice. You can request that funds be made immediately available. If the bank is not willing to comply with your request, and these three days make a substantial difference to your cash flow, you can move your account to another bank.

Use a financing company

If you turn your customers over to a financing company to allow them to pay for your product or service over time, they will be more inclined to buy your product or service and you will get your money immediately. You can even create and run the financing company as a separate entity. The financing company's profits are made on the interest the customer pays. So now your company could generate two types of revenue — one from selling a product or service and one from financing the purchase. Revenues from financing arrangements are critical to the success of department stores and car dealerships.

Invoice as frequently as possible

Do not wait. As soon as the item is shipped or the service is provided, start the process for collections. I've run into several service businesses that only bill once a month. This means that many of the services are benefiting the client for 30 days before the bill is even out. Even increasing billing to semi-monthly could make a huge difference in cash flow.

Pre-bill where you can

It is common practice in the advertising business for customers to pay up front. Advertisers and graphic artists bill 30% at sale, 30% at draft stage, 30% at delivery and 10% on terms after delivery. This way they have 90% of their money by the time the ad goes out or the collateral is created.

Ask for payments more frequently

My mortgage company recently sent me a very interesting letter. I wonder how many people went for it. They said in the letter that they would be happy to do me the favor of taking my mortgage payment out of my checking account two times a month for a mere $400 registration fee. If I did this, I would pay off my home quicker. No, thank you. First of all, I would not give the mortgage company access to my bank account — what a nightmare that could cause. And secondly, I could pay off the mortgage myself every two weeks if I wanted to. I didn't need their assistance.

Bill when customers are most likely to pay

You may know when your customer is flush with money and best able to pay you. Electric utilities often use this technique, billing elderly clients around the time their Social Security check arrives.

Send out statements

Statements have the power to both remind and confuse. I worked in an accounts payable department of a large manufacturer when I was in college and I remember spending a lot of time reconciling individual bills to monthly statements to make sure that we were all caught up with the vendor. I was often told by my supervisor to wait to receive the statement before paying.

I think it might be a better idea to just send each invoice that needs to be paid individually and skip sending statements. Whether you use the statement depends on what your customer needs to be able to pay you. If they like statements, use them. If you are the one that likes statements and the customers hate them, stop sending them out — they are likely holding up your payment.

Limit terms

Do not allow your salespeople to use extended terms as a negotiating tool in their sales pitches. Some salespeople might promise the customer a product today and allow them to pay much later. Sometimes 60 to 90 days later. This is good if they are racking up sales, but bad if you are interested in collecting early or even within a reasonable time frame.

Invoice correctly

An incorrect invoice can severely delay payment. The customer won't call you and complain, they will just wait for you to call wanting your money and THEN they'll tell you the problem. Best to get it right the first time.

Understand what the payer needs in order to pay

Some of my clients need certain information on the invoice before they can process it for payment. For instance, I might need to include a PO number or my Tax ID# on the invoice. I might also have to send them multiple copies of the invoice — sending one to the purchaser, one to accounts payable, and one to education services. I have found over time it is better to get it right the first time to speed payment. I ask the customer, "What do I need to send you in order to get paid?" And then I can simply comply with what they need.

Educate clients about your expectations

Tell the clients as you make a sale about your expectation to be paid in 30 days or less and remind them again and again. Write it down in bold on your invoices, post it on your wall, and send them a letter establishing the ground rules.

Call or email frequently

Call the customer often. You can call them after you send the invoice to make sure they got it. You can call them a few days later to make sure that they don't need any more information to process the invoice. Call them a few days before the payment is due to remind them that it is due. Call them on the due date to tell them it is due. They will pay you just to stop hearing from you. (They may also take their business elsewhere if you are too irritating.)

Get a proof of delivery

I've heard more than a few horror stories about big-name retailers who take delivery of products, sell the products, and then tell the vendor that they never received the goods! So much for trust, huh? Forget trust! Get proof in writing from your customer that they received the items.

Get a PO because it is a contractual obligation

Again, if you are worried that your customer may decide not to pay you after you have provided them with a product or service, document their commitment to you in writing. A purchase order will stand up in case of dispute and show that the client did indeed commit to paying for your goods or services.

Differentiate your product so that they will think twice about paying late

If you have something that no one else has, and the customer wants your product or service again, they may think twice about not paying you.

Screen customers for credit worthiness

Screen potential clients for their credit worthiness. Some customers do not deserve credit because they may never pay. The customers with poor credit should be required to pay up front. You can subscribe to a credit rating service to help you determine whether customers are credit worthy or not. These services range in prices and in quality. A few you may want to check out include Dunn & Bradstreet, Moody's, and Standard & Poor's.

Have salespeople profile customers

Salespeople can be your first line of defense against bad customers. They are often closest to the customer and will be able to spot trouble sooner than your accountant will. Have them fill out a profile of each customer they do business with. If you combine this with the idea of only giving them commissions when the sale is collected, you may prevent bad sales from being made in the first place.

Reward salespeople for collections

Instead of only rewarding salespeople when they make a sale, add a component that rewards them when their customer finally pays. You may even want to make this the main criteria for bonuses and commissions. The salesperson will work to qualify customers and won't make a quick sale if they do not think the customer is credit worthy. Some companies even penalize salespeople for making bad sales by taking back their commission plus 20%.

Purchase credit insurance

If you have a group of clients who worry you, yet you still want to do business with them — you might consider purchasing credit insurance. One reseller of manufacturing equipment does a lot of business in Mexico and often purchase credit insurance on questionable but large accounts receivable. The premiums have been worth it because the insurance has paid on delinquent accounts several times.

Take a lien

On large items, you may take a lien out on the item or something the product or service attaches to. For instance, if you are a plumber working on a new house and the contractor does not pay you for your work, you can put a lien on the house and when it goes to closing, either the buyer or the seller (contractor) must pay you.

Have the customers sign change orders

Every time the client wants a change from standard offerings, it should be clearly documented and priced. In this way, if there is a dispute, you have the full amount of the receivable documented.

Use collection agents

Once an item has been outstanding for a while, you can hire a collections agent to get some of your money back. Because collection agents are so expensive, often taking up to 50% of the receivable amount, you want to make every effort on your own before resorting to this method. But 50% is better than nothing!

Sell uncollected accounts receivable

Sometimes a factoring agent may agree to buy your uncollected receivables for pennies on the dollar. When the customer does pay, they pay the factoring agent instead of you. This is an expensive way to get cash quick — as you might pay over 15% interest for the privilege. Again, you must determine if immediate liquidity is worth taking the hit on the amount you collect.

Use repo agents

Depending on what sort of business you run, it might be appropriate to hire "Guidos" or repossession experts to help you either get your money or your goods back. The personal touch, as it were.

Cut off services

If the customer doesn't pay — you can and should cut their services off. My sister monitors service contracts for a software company. If the customer pays her a monthly fee, she will update them on the latest changes to the software. If the customer does not pay, she instructs her technical support people not to talk to that particular client. She is firm on this policy — but she has moved many slow payers to mail that check!

Review aging reports
with managers and salespeople

Generate accounts receivable aging reports and track the progress of client payments. Review the report with the folks in your organization that have a relationship with these clients — the service providers or the salespeople — and have them follow up with delinquent or late customers. Bonus them for collections.

Sell COD

Do not allow receivables at all. Ask for cash on delivery. This can be arranged with your freight company.

Accept credit cards

Credit cards pay in three days. The only problem with credit cards is you have to have a system for accepting them AND you pay a little fee every time your customer uses them for a transaction. You can pay up to a 4% fee for using credit cards and if your margins are already low, this is a high price to pay.

If it gets measured, it gets done

Give your staff bonuses for getting the accounts receivable in quicker. Use a metric — such as the number of days sales are outstanding — to track your progress in getting your money in faster. Whoever is involved in making receivables come in faster should get a cut of the pie.

Chapter 10:
Ideas for Stretching Payments to Vendors

This is probably one of the easiest working capital items to manage. It just takes a decision to stretch payments to vendors, and vigilance. But as you can imagine, stretching payables to vendors can have very negative consequences. If you stretch beyond the number of days standard in your industry, you run the risk of at best annoying your vendors and at worst killing your vendor's business. So be very careful with this one. This is an area where you may be tempted to compromise your ethics.

Here are some ideas — use each with care and with full awareness of the impact it has on your vendor relationships. They need cash to run their business, too!

Use remote accounts to disburse funds

To add a few days to the time it takes vendors to receive payment, you can instruct a bank on the other side of the country to pay your bill on the day the bill is due. That way, the payment is dated as of the due date but the two days it takes for the mail to travel across the country stalls the actual deposit. This technique is commonly called "mail float."

Hold stacks of checks for later payment

I use this trick myself. I write checks for every bill that comes into my office when I receive it and I write the date it is due on the outside of the envelope. I sort the outgoing mail in a stack in date order and then mail the payments as necessary.

Lose the invoice

This is a joke. But sadly, it is a technique that many companies use to avoid — at least temporarily — their responsibility to pay. One company I contracted with would throw any erroneous invoice in the garbage. After waiting the standard 30 days, I called them and they informed me of my error. They said they would start the 30 days ticking again after they received the corrected invoice. By being so persnickety, they stretched several of my payments out by two or more months.

Create a hierarchy or schedule of payments

One experienced CFO uses what he calls a hierarchy of payment schedule. When presented with a stack of bills to pay, he always pays payroll first because he wouldn't want to lose an employee! Then he pays rent and makes loan payments. If he has any cash left, he pays utilities so that the electricity and phone will keep working, and then he pays critical vendors. Non-critical vendors — such as consultants or trainers providing a one-time service — get paid next. And lastly, he pays the attorneys. He reasons that if the attorneys can wait so long to bill and have such a bad internal process for tracking receivables, he shouldn't worry about stretching them out a few more days.

Net payments when vendors are also customers

Some of your vendors may also be your customers. Instead of you paying them and then waiting for them to pay you, net the payable and the receivable. Reduce the amount of your payment to them by the amount they owe you.

Negotiate for longer terms

In your contracts with vendors, tell them that you will not be paying in 30 days, but in 45, 60, or 80 days instead. If they sign the contract, they have accepted the terms and you can pay them at a later time without any guilt. The more purchasing clout you have, the more leeway your vendors will give you. For instance, both Dell and Wal-Mart stretch their payables beyond 80 days.

Pay with credit cards

As mentioned earlier, one florist I met was able to stretch her payables by using credit cards. Her major flower supplier billed her once a month. She waited until the last day possible to pay the bill and then paid it with a credit card. She would then wait for the credit card bill and pay the bill on the last possible day. Using this technique, everyone was happy and she was able to stretch her payables out without incurring a finance charge.

Pay a little bit on outstanding balances

If you pay a bit here and a bit there, the vendor will feel better and have some cash flow even if they do not have the full amount.

Be consistent in your lateness

Maybe you could stretch your payment out beyond terms but then consistently pay late around the same time. For instance, if terms are net 30, stretch your payments to 45 days and do it consistently. The vendor may get used to your behavior and feel comforted knowing they will get the money. Of course, you only want to do this if there isn't a big penalty involved for late payment.

Use excuses

Old standbys include "The check is in the mail", "I'm sick", and the best excuse ever, "The dog ate my homework."

Take major vendor discounts even if you pay late

If you are offered a discount, you may decide to take it even if you pay late. This is a rough tactic, but one that many big businesses use.

Form a friendly relationship with vendors

A friend of mine who owns a marble and granite installation company travels all the way from Texas to Italy every year to meet with his suppliers. He actually doesn't like to travel, but feels that meeting with his suppliers is critical to the success of his business. He wants to make sure that he has a good relationship with the quarries and craftsmen so that he can make special requests and have some leeway on payables.

Instead of hiding out hoping that the vendor does not bother you about the payment, open the lines of communication and give them a heads up when you think you might be stretching payments. Let them know when cash is tight and reassure them they will get their money. When you are flush with money, give them their money a little bit early to return the favor.

Epilogue: Choose

A final thought.

One of my favorite sayings is:

> **There are no answers, only choices.**

This book has given you ideas that may change the course of your business. What you do with the information is up to you — it is a choice. Some of the ideas you implement will work like a charm and your cash flow problems will disappear. Others may help your cash flow but cause other unintended effects.

The great thing about business is that you have the ability to back up or to undo most choices that you make. If you see that something is not working for you, you can change your mind and change your business.

I would love to hear from you about the choices you have made based on the ideas in this book. Please write to me at Leita@leitahart.com and let me hear your stories.

Appendix A: Calculating the Metrics

To compare your DSO, DSI, and DPO metrics to other businesses in your same industry, go to CFO.com — the website for *CFO Magazine* — and locate this article in the September 2003 issue: "Barely Working: the 2003 Working Capital Survey." The article ranks the top 500 companies and is performed every fall.

The formulas for the metrics are:

–DPO

Accounts Payable/Daily Payments Made

+DSI

Average Inventory/(Cost of Goods Sold/365)

+DSO

Average Accounts Receivable/(Net Sales/365)

Please keep in mind that your direct knowledge should come into play here. If the number you get from the formulas seems way off base, it probably is.

Each is easily estimated without a fancy formula. You know how long it takes you to pay your vendors — that is your DPO. You can easily find out how long it takes to collect from your customers by doing an accounts receivable aging report from your general ledger. And the age of your inventory can be likened to your inventory turns, or the number of times per year you have to restock. If you have to restock each month, then the days' supply of inventory is 30.

Appendix B: A Simple Cash Flow Projection Tool

Cash and profit are two totally different things. Remember the story of my engineer friend in the introduction, the guy who made global positioning systems? He made the mistake of thinking that everything that was on the income statement was in his bank account.

This will never be true if you use the accrual basis of accounting. And most of us do. If you have receivables and payables, you are using the accrual method of accounting. The alternative method is the cash basis of accounting.

A hot dog vendor on the street will use the cash basis of accounting. Every morning, he hooks his little cart up to his truck and drives over to the grocery store to buy wieners, buns, and condiments. He pays cash.

That day at lunch, he sells his hot dogs for cash. At night, he eats the leftover hot dogs and starts again fresh the next day. It is all about cash. Cash paid and cash collected.

Now in accrual accounting, you record things before they happen. For instance, you make a sale, but do not collect it in cash. The customer will pay you in 30 days. This transaction is recorded on the income statement but has no effect on cash flow. No money has been received yet. Only when cash is collected do we have money to spend in our bank account.

We can also incur expenses but not pay them in cash. These expenses are recorded on the income statement as accounts payable, but do not affect cash until they are paid.

So, the first thing I counseled my engineer friend to do was to watch the cash flow statement instead of the income statement. Both statements are useful, but the accounts receivables recorded on the income statement do not pay payroll on Friday. Only cash does.

For a few months, he projected cash flow on a daily basis. Once he got a sense of the timing of receipts and disbursements, he moved to a weekly forecast, and then a monthly forecast.

Here is what he did for each day of the upcoming week:

	M	T	W	T	F
How much cash did I have this morning?	100	90	80	125	135
How much cash am I going to collect and deposit in the bank today?	20	0	50	10	20
How much cash am I going to pay out to vendors, employees, and others?	(30)	(10)	(5)	0	(90)
How much cash will I have free at the end of the day?	90	80	125	135	65

So, you just add beginning cash to cash collected and subtract out cash paid.

This way if he saw that on Thursday night he did not have enough money left in his account to meet payroll on Friday, he could draw from his credit line at the bank or ask his partners to chip in from their personal accounts. This way, he was not surprised on Friday morning when he didn't have cash in the bank account and his employees were not surprised when their checks bounced.

A Few Nuances
of the Cash Flow Projection

I need to warn you of a few of the nuances of this statement. If you are tracking cash on a daily basis, you are going to run into some timing differences in dealing with the bank. First off, the bank will not make all of your deposits available to you on the day you deposit them. They may put your deposits on hold until they are sure the checks deposited don't bounce.

Also, any checks you write may take a while to clear. Maybe your vendor is on the other side of the country and it takes two days for the mail to reach them and then another three days for them to deposit the funds. This means you have the cash in your account for five extra days after you write a check.

So, the money you deposited may not be available to you and the money you paid out may not be gone from your bank account!

What do you do about this? Well, you can estimate when things are going to hit your account and adjust the projection to actual on a regular basis.

But only if you are in a tight cash crunch do you have to worry about cash flow on a *daily* basis. In most cases, a two-week projection will suffice. Many of the timing differences with the bank I just described will even out over a two-week period.

The frequency and accuracy of financial information will cost you time and money. You have to decide how much the information is worth to you.

For my business, I pay my bills every two weeks and know, in general, how much I pay out each time. I also keep a running list of the folks that owe me money and when I billed them. Some of my clients pay in two weeks, some in 30 days, and some in 60+ days.

Using this knowledge, I can predict how much money I will have in the bank every two weeks for the next few months. I can see when I will have to temporarily move cash from my reserve account into my checking account to cover my bill payments when I see that the clients that owe me money will not likely pay in time to cover the expenses.

If I was only looking at my income statement, I might assume that I was rich. Sometimes I have tens of thousands of dollars in receivables but only a few thousand in my bank account. Unfortunately, the profit on my income statement will not pay my bills . . . why? Because it isn't cash yet!

.

Leita Hart, CPA

Leita Hart makes finance fun and easy. She converts the complex topics of accounting, finance, auditing, and strategic planning into information that professionals can absorb and use.

Leita has owned and operated Leita Hart CPA & Associates, a training and professional development company, since 1995. She has conducted and developed courses on balanced scorecard management, audit supervision, budgeting, business writing, finance for non-financial managers, cash flow, presentation skills, government auditing standards, and client relations.

Leita's clients include Dell Computer, First Data Corporation, the Texas Society of CPAs, Great West Life Insurance, USAA, the National Association of State Auditor's, Comptrollers, and Treasurers, the University of Texas, Holt, Rinehart & Winston, Steck Vaughn Publishers, the Texas State Auditor's Office, Broadwing, Inc., the Association of Government Accountants, the Texas Natural Resource Conservation Commission, The Alaska State Auditor, Western CPE, The Montana Society of CPAs, The

Pennsylvania Comptroller, the Texas Department of Human Services, the Louisiana Department of Transportation, Texas State University, The Minnesota Society of CPAs, the Arizona Society of CPAs, and the Texas Department of Protective and Regulatory Services.

Leita is a graduate of the University of Texas at Austin. She is a Certified Public Accountant and a Certified Government Financial Manager. She is a member of the Association of Government Accountants, the Southwest Intergovernmental Audit Forum, and the American Society of Training and Development. She also serves on the board of the local chapter of the National Speakers Association.

Leita is the author of *STEP by STEP: Building Persuasive Audit Reports* and *The Four Principles of Happy Cash Flow™*.

Please visit her website at www.leitahart.com.

The Four Principles of Happy Cash Flow™

1. Use Other People's Money

In other words, make sure to pay your payables late, keep inventory low, and get your money from your customers as fast as possible.

2. Cut the Number of Days

Here, you want to cut the number of days that your money is tied up unnecessarily in receivables and inventory, and increase the number of days you hold on to your money in the form of payables. We covered three metrics to measure the number of days in the cycle — DSO, DSI, and DPO.

3. Pump Up the Volume

The more transactions you run through your now efficient cash conversion cycle, the better.

4. Put a Little In, Get a Lot Out

Increase your profit margins by selling at the maximum price and spending as little as possible to create your product or service. You may have to apply the McDonald's "Want fries with that?" concept to keep margins high overall.